Growing Herbs for Beginners

A Comprehensive Guide to Herbal Gardening and Growing Your Own Medicinal and Culinary Herbs

David Werner

Copyright

Copyright ©2024 David Werner. All rights reserved

Table of content

COPYRIGHT

ABSTRACT

INTRODUCTION

Chapter 1: Why Grow Your Own Herbs?

Chapter 2: Benefits of growing your own herbs

Chapter 3: Cooking with Herbs

Chapter 4: Herb Garden Design - Choosing A Site For Your Herb Garden

- Sunlight for Your Herb Garden
- Well-Drained Soil for Your Herb Garden
- Location of Herb Gardens
- Selecting the right herbs for your garden
- Considerations for Selecting Herbs
- Best Culinary Herbs to Grow
- Best Medicinal Herbs to Grow
- Preparing the Soil

Chapter 5: How To Grow Herbs From Seed Successfully Every Time

- 5 Essential Tips For Growing Herbs From Seed
- Essential Supplies to Grow Herbs From Seeds
- What are Some of the Fastest Growing Herbs from Seed?
- What Is The Right Herb Growing Temperature?
- Which Herb Seeds Need Light To Germinate?
- How Far Apart to Plant your Herb Seeds?

- Labeling Your Herb Garden Seeds
- Transplanting Herbs

Chapter 6: Providing Adequate Water

- 7 Watering Tips For Herbs

Chapter 7: Fertilizing the Herbs

Chapter 8: HOW TO PRUNE HERBS FOR THE BEST AND FRESHEST RESULTS

Chapter 9: How to Harvest Herbs so That the Leaves Keep on Coming

- The 3 Rules of Harvesting Herbs
- Rule 1: Use a Clean Pair Of Pruners Or Scissors
- Rule 2: Harvest When The Leaves Are Dry
- Rule 3: Keep The Golden Rule In Mind
- When to Harvest Annual Herbs
- How to Harvest Annual Herbs
- How To Harvest Cilantro, Dill, & Parsley
- How To Harvest Basil
- How to Enjoy Your Annual Herbs
- How To Enjoy Cilantro, Dill & Parsley
- How To Enjoy Basil
- When to Harvest Perennial Herbs
- How to Harvest Perennial Herbs
- How to Enjoy Perennial Herbs
- How to Enjoy Sage
- How to Enjoy Rosemary
- How to Enjoy Mint
- How to Enjoy Thyme
- How to Enjoy Oregano

Chapter 10: Protecting from Pests and Diseases

Chapter 11: Culinary Herbs

1. Anise
2. Basil
3. Bay
4. Borage
5. Caraway
6. Chamomile
7. Chervil
8. Chives
9. Cilantro/Coriander
10. Cumin

Chapter 12: Medicinal Herbs

1. Angelica
2. Bee Balm, or Bergamot
3 Echinacea, or Coneflower
4. Fenugreek
5. Garlic
6. Ginger
7. Jasmine
8. Lavender 9. Lemongrass

10. Red Clover

Abstract

Embark on a journey into the world of herbal gardening with our comprehensive guide tailored for beginners. Learn the essentials of cultivating your own medicinal and culinary herbs, from selecting the right plants to nurturing them to maturity. Unlock the secrets of successful herb growing and elevate your gardening skills.

INTRODUCTION

Embarking on the Journey of Growing Your Own Herbs

Growing your own food can be a transformative experience, sparking a sense of wonder and connection to the natural world. Whether it was witnessing your grandfather's garden flourish or nurturing a potted basil plant to culinary success, the realization of one's ability to cultivate sustenance is truly magical. In a society often distanced from the agricultural process, cultivating edible plants becomes not only a therapeutic endeavor but also a revolutionary act.

For those eager to delve into the realm of home gardening but unsure where to begin, herbs serve as an accessible entry point. Widely available and versatile, herbs beckon from the shelves of hardware stores and nurseries, offering an array of options from common staples like basil and parsley to more exotic varieties like tarragon and nettle. Moreover, herbs boast adaptability, thriving in diverse climates with minimal maintenance requirements. Whether one's gardening space is confined to a city balcony or sprawls across acres of land, herbs promise contentment and growth.

Embarking on this journey entails more than just planting seeds; it involves nurturing plants through every stage of growth, from fertilization to harvesting. Our comprehensive guide covers the essentials, empowering enthusiasts to cultivate not only herbs but also their well-being. Join us as we share our passion for herb gardening and the joy of fostering health from the ground up.

Chapter 1

Why Grow Your Own Herbs?

Venturing into the world of herb gardening may initially appear excessive to some, particularly when these green companions are readily available in grocery stores. However, investing time and effort into nurturing herbs can offer profound rewards, extending beyond mere culinary convenience.

Discovering the Therapeutic Value

Engaging in gardening activities can serve as a therapeutic respite from the hustle and bustle of daily life. Research conducted by a Texas A&M AgriLife Extension Service specialist reveals that gardening fosters increased self-esteem, uplifts mood, mitigates anger, and diminishes levels of anxiety and depression. Furthermore, a study conducted at the University of Colorado Boulder suggests that exposure to soil microorganisms can enhance stress resilience and mitigate the risk of mood disorders. Thus, herb cultivation not only yields nutritional benefits but also contributes to mental well-being.

Embracing Sustainability

The sustainability aspect of herb cultivation warrants consideration. While growing a single herb may not significantly impact global ecological challenges, every small effort contributes to alleviating strain on the planet's food systems, which face mounting pressure due to population growth and climate change. Additionally, cultivating herbs like rosemary, thyme, cilantro, dill, and lavender can provide vital resources to essential pollinators such as bees and butterflies, bolstering biodiversity and minimizing reliance on harmful pesticides. Ultimately, engaging in herb gardening transcends personal health and taste preferences, presenting an opportunity to positively influence the surrounding environment.

Chapter 2

Benefits of growing your own herbs

In the tranquil mornings of Florida, except for the sweltering summer months, I routinely step onto my porch to pluck fresh chives for my breakfast. This simple act underscores the unparalleled access to organic herbs that home gardening offers, far surpassing the offerings of a grocery store. Maintaining my herb garden not only grants me the liberty to harvest as needed but also facilitates savings and reduces wastage. Given its simplicity, I highly recommend herb gardening to novice cultivators, regardless of their living situation.

1. Ideal for Novice Gardeners

While I cherish my vegetable garden, I firmly believe that herb gardening stands as the ideal starting point for beginners. It demands minimal effort to initiate and is remarkably forgiving in its growth requirements. Moreover, the gratification of consuming homegrown herbs adds to their appeal.

Simplicity of Cultivation

Herb cultivation proves simpler than nurturing vegetables and, in some cases, even flowers. They adapt well to various environments, thriving indoors, in pots, or directly in the soil. Innovative solutions like hydroponic kits further simplify indoor herb cultivation, exemplified by products such as the AeroGarden. Personally, I favor pot cultivation on my porch, benefiting from the morning sun. With minimal fertilization needs and a tolerance for diverse temperatures, herbs offer a hassle-free gardening experience. A mere stroll to the porch yields fresh chives for my scrambled eggs each morning.

Ease of Initiation

Launching an herb garden requires minimal effort, constituting one of its primary advantages. Whether starting from seeds or transplants, herbs exhibit resilience to transplantation, providing instant access to fresh produce. Multiple herbs can thrive in a single pot, making it feasible even for those without extensive outdoor space, such as apartment dwellers. A pot, some soil, and seeds or transplants are all that's necessary to embark on this journey. This contrasts with vegetable gardens, which demand more substantial space investments for a satisfactory yield. Transplants or seeds are readily available at nurseries, home improvement stores like Lowes or Home Depot, and online platforms.

2. Enhances Well-being
Promoting Physical Health

Cultivating your own herb garden opens avenues for incorporating fresh, organic herbs into your diet, thereby bolstering your health in multifaceted ways.

Herbs serve as allies in fortifying the immune system, aiding detoxification, and alleviating common ailments such as colds, digestive issues, headaches, and stress.

Herbs as Vital Nutrients

Beyond their culinary allure, herbs harbor an array of health benefits for the body. Medicinal herbs can be harnessed through various means, including teas, tinctures, essential oils, and salves. Examples of medicinal herbs encompass calendula, chamomile, echinacea, feverfew, goldenrod, lavender, lemon balm, oregano, peppermint, St. John's-wort, and yarrow. Notable herbs like peppermint uplift mood, enhance focus, soothe nausea, and aid digestion, while oregano's antioxidant-rich profile bolsters immunity and exhibits antifungal and antibacterial properties. Cilantro, renowned for its detoxifying prowess against heavy metals, stands as another exemplary herb.

Embracing the Therapeutic Garden

Engaging in garden maintenance offers more than just physical health benefits—it fosters holistic well-being. Tending to your garden provides opportunities for physical activity, fresh air, exposure to vitamin D, and exercise, all of which contribute to a healthier lifestyle. Furthermore, gardening serves as a therapeutic escape from the rigors of modern life, allowing individuals to disconnect from technology and immerse themselves in a calming, hands-on activity.

3. Economical Advantages

Establishing an herb garden presents a practical approach to economizing. The cost-effectiveness of growing herbs surpasses that of purchasing them, leading to substantial savings in the long run. While initial investment in vegetable gardening may entail higher startup costs and a steeper learning curve, herb cultivation remains relatively inexpensive. A single packet of herb seeds, priced at a few dollars, can sustain herb production for years, with the potential for indefinite growth through seed saving practices.

Reduced Food Waste
In addition to financial savings, herb gardening minimizes food wastage—an ethical and practical concern for conscientious consumers. Unlike store-bought herbs, which often perish before complete utilization, homegrown herbs allow for selective harvesting, reducing excess and enhancing sustainability. By cultivating herbs, individuals mitigate unnecessary food waste, aligning with principles of mindful consumption and environmental stewardship.

4. Ensures Fresh Herb Supply
Embarking on herb cultivation guarantees a level of freshness that surpasses store-bought alternatives. Have you ever scrutinized the condition of herbs purchased from a local grocery store? It's a common plight to encounter wilted leaves, a testament to the

significant duration between harvest and purchase. Store-bought herbs endure days, if not weeks, of transit and storage, often compromising their integrity upon reaching consumers. This predicament is exacerbated for those seeking organic options, where quality may further deteriorate over time. The frustration of investing in herbs only to find them half-wilted upon use is all too familiar.

Enhancing Culinary Experiences

Beyond mere freshness, homegrown herbs elevate culinary experiences by infusing dishes with vibrant flavors. Unlike their store-bought counterparts, freshly picked herbs retain maximum flavor and nutritional potency. The immediacy of plucking organic herbs moments before incorporation into a recipe imparts a distinct freshness unparalleled by mass-produced alternatives. Basil, chives, cilantro, dill, oregano, parsley, rosemary, sage, and thyme—these culinary treasures impart depth and complexity to dishes, transforming ordinary meals into culinary delights.

5. Educational Enrichment

The act of cultivating herbs extends beyond mere horticulture—it serves as a dynamic educational tool for both adults and children alike. For children, herb gardening offers invaluable lessons in food origins, instilling an appreciation for the effort and resources involved in food production. This firsthand connection to the growth process cultivates healthy eating habits, encourages environmental consciousness, and fosters a sense of responsibility towards sustainable practices. Involving children in garden maintenance not only promotes family bonding but also nurtures practical skills and environmental stewardship.

Life Lessons for Adults

The educational benefits of herb cultivation extend to adults, imparting profound insights into patience, resilience, and the unpredictability of outcomes.

The journey from seed to harvest parallels life's journey, wherein perseverance and resilience often yield unexpected rewards. Waiting for vegetables to mature teaches patience, while confronting setbacks cultivates resilience and adaptability. The garden thus emerges as a metaphorical classroom, offering invaluable lessons in lifelong learning and personal growth.

Chapter 3

Cooking with Herbs

Harnessing the transformative power of fresh herbs can elevate any dish, infusing it with vibrant flavors and aromatic nuances.

Accessible Herb Cultivation
Herb cultivation transcends geographical constraints, thriving in urban apartments or spacious countryside gardens alike. Whether nestled in a window-box, terracotta pot, or makeshift bucket, herbs promise an endless supply of culinary enhancements.

Understanding Herb Varieties

Herbs are categorized into woody and soft varieties, each imparting distinctive flavors and culinary uses. Woody herbs like rosemary and thyme lend robustness to cooked dishes, while soft herbs like basil, coriander, and parsley offer fresh, delicate notes suitable for salads and garnishes.

Exploring Common Herbs

Basil: A staple of Italian cuisine, basil's sweet, slightly aniseed flavor complements pasta dishes, salads, and pesto. Its versatility extends to pairing with eggs, tomatoes, mozzarella, and seafood, offering endless culinary possibilities.

Chives: With a delicate onion flavor, chives enhance salads, savory dishes, and breakfast fare like eggs on toast, adding a refreshing touch to culinary creations.

Oregano: A soft herb with a robust flavor, oregano enriches red meats, pasta dishes, and slow-cooked vegetables, embodying the essence of Italian and Italian-American cuisine.

Marjoram: Resembling oregano but with thinner leaves, marjoram enriches northern European dishes, pairing harmoniously with root vegetables, pork, and baked fish.

Parsley: Whether flat-leaf or curly, parsley serves as the quintessential garnish, enhancing rich dishes like roasted meats, fish, and omelets with its bitter yet fresh flavor.

Mint: A resilient herb available in varieties like peppermint and spearmint, mint lends its refreshing essence to fruit salads, grilled fruits, cocktails, and savory dishes, offering a burst of freshness in every bite.

Rosemary:

Rosemary, classified as a woody herb, boasts sturdy leaves ideal for dishes with prolonged cooking times. Often utilized in conjunction with roast meats, roasted potatoes, and bread like focaccia, rosemary imparts a fragrant, earthy flavor profile. Its versatile stalks serve as flavor enhancers in soups, stews, and even as skewers for grilling kebabs. Additionally, rosemary harmonizes seamlessly with gin, as showcased in tantalizing cocktail recipes.

Thyme:

Characterized by its robust bush and delicate, aromatic leaves, thyme is a staple in stews, stocks, and slow-cooked dishes. Its versatile nature extends to roasted meats, vegetables, and cheesy bakes like mac 'n' cheese. However, due to its potent flavor, thyme is best used sparingly to avoid overwhelming other ingredients.

Sage:

Resilient and aromatic, sage thrives in various weather conditions and enhances dishes with its intense flavor. Unlike parsley's sharpness, sage amplifies surrounding flavors, making it an ideal companion for dishes like bangers and mash, English onion soup, or pork chops.

Coriander:

With its citrusy, sweet undertones, coriander serves as a vibrant garnish for finished dishes, particularly in Latin American, Mexican, and Asian cuisines. Whether incorporated into guacamole, ceviche, or Asian curries, coriander adds a refreshing twist. Its stalks, rich in flavor, are essential in curry pastes and contribute depth to culinary creations.

Dill:

Distinct from fennel, dill imparts a fragrant aroma and pairs exquisitely with fish, especially smoked salmon. Popular in Eastern European cuisine, dill enhances salads, potatoes, eggs, and carrots, showcasing its versatility and delicate flavor profile.

Sorrel:

Featuring a lemony sourness, sorrel enhances cooked dishes, particularly those involving eggs, fish, and goat's cheese. Its acidity enlivens potato and grain salads, contributing a refreshing zest to seasonal English fare.

Tarragon:

Delicate tarragon, reminiscent of aniseed, complements chicken, eggs, tomatoes, and potatoes with its subtle flavor. Its long, floppy leaves add a touch of elegance to dishes, enhancing their visual appeal alongside their taste.

Chervil:

Similar to tarragon but milder in flavor, chervil boasts delicate leaves perfect for salads and lightly flavored soups. Chefs often utilize chervil leaves as garnishes, elevating dishes with their delicate appearance and subtle taste.

Chapter 4

Herb Garden Design - Choosing A Site For Your Herb Garden

When determining the ideal location for your herb garden, there are several crucial factors to weigh before settling on a permanent spot.

Sunlight Requirements

Prioritize selecting a site that basks in sunlight for at least six to eight hours daily. Sunlight is essential for the optimal growth and development of most herbs. Lack of adequate sunlight can result in leggy, underproductive plants. Survey your yard to identify sunny spots, considering the impact of trees, structures, and tall plants that may cast shadows at different times of the day. While some herbs tolerate shade, their options for culinary use are limited. Container gardening is a viable solution if sunlight is scarce, allowing for easy relocation to capture the required sunlight.

Soil Quality

Herbs thrive in well-drained, light soil conducive to cultivation. Assess the soil quality at your chosen site by running water and observing drainage. If water accumulates, amend the soil with sand, peat, or compost to enhance drainage. Caution must be exercised with compost, as overly rich soil can weaken herbs and make them susceptible to diseases. Aim for a pH level around 6.5, although most herbs tolerate slight acidity or alkalinity. Moderate fertilization is typically sufficient for optimal growth.

Accessibility and Practicality

Consider practicality when determining the garden's location to ensure convenience and usability. Opt for a site within easy reach to facilitate harvesting and maintenance tasks. Placing the herb garden near your back door enables effortless access and allows you to savor the aromatic scents wafting from the garden. Alternatively, integrating herbs among shrubs and flowers in the front yard enhances aesthetics while maintaining accessibility. Proximity to the house simplifies watering, pruning, and tending to the herbs, fostering a flourishing and functional garden.

Investing time in selecting the optimal site for your herb garden guarantees a productive, accessible, and visually appealing outdoor space, enhancing your culinary endeavors and garden enjoyment.

Choosing the Perfect Herbs for Your Garden

Cultivating herbs in your garden brings forth a myriad of advantages, from infusing your culinary creations with fresh, aromatic flavors to offering natural remedies for various health concerns (as always, consider the appropriate cautions). Below, we delve into popular herbs well-suited for home gardens, alongside key considerations for selection and tips for successful growth.

Factors to Weigh When Selecting Herbs

When deciding on herbs for your garden, take into account local growing conditions, climate suitability, space availability, and intended use, whether culinary or medicinal. Certain herbs thrive in specific environments, emphasizing the importance of selecting plants aligned with your garden's unique conditions.

Top Culinary Herbs for Cultivation

Basil: Renowned for its versatility and fragrance, basil thrives in warm, sunny locations. Its presence is prominent in Italian cuisine, enriching dishes like pesto and caprese salad. Varieties such as Genovese and Italian Large Leaf are highly recommended.

Parsley: Flourishing in well-drained soil and full sunlight, parsley is valued both as a garnish and a flavor enhancer in soups, stews, and sauces. The AAS winner Evergreen Parsley is a preferred choice.

Dill: With its delicate, tender parts, dill is a popular culinary herb, finely chopped for sauces and used fresh in pickling. Bouquet Dill is a recommended variety.

Thyme: Exhibiting versatility across various conditions, thyme enriches dishes ranging from roasted meats to soups. Garden Thyme is a recommended choice.

Oregano: Preferring well-drained soil and ample sunlight, oregano is a staple in Italian and Greek cuisines, featuring prominently in pizza and pasta sauces.

Finest Medicinal Herbs for Cultivation
Valerian: A resilient perennial herb, Valerian thrives in full sun and moist, well-drained soils, boasting a medicinal legacy dating back centuries.

Chamomile: Preferring full sun to partial shade, chamomile is prized for its calming properties and finds utility in teas and remedies for relaxation and digestion.

Echinacea: Known for immune-boosting properties, Echinacea prefers full sun and well-draining soil, attracting butterflies and other pollinators.

Feverfew: Celebrated for its ornamental blooms and medicinal value, feverfew flourishes in full sun and is utilized in traditional teas and medicinal preparations.

Hyssop: Hailing from Southern Europe and the Middle East, hyssop has a long history of medicinal use, making it a noteworthy addition to herb gardens.

Special Mention: Medicinal Herbs Garden Pack
For comprehensive medicinal herb cultivation, consider our Medicinal Herbs Garden Pack, featuring a selection of our most popular medicinal herbs.

Soil Preparation for Herb Gardening
Aside from essentials like watering, feeding, and sunlight, the soil plays a pivotal role in nurturing your herb garden. Serving as the foundation of your garden or container, soil quality dictates the growth and vitality of your herbs. It's crucial to

comprehend, nourish, and maintain your soil for the optimal health of your herbs.

While many herbs thrive in typical garden soil with adequate drainage, Mediterranean natives prefer gritty, well-drained conditions. Poor drainage can lead to root rot, particularly in moist soil. For heavy garden soil, consider growing these herbs in containers or raised beds akin to those found in Jekka's Herbetum.

Understanding your soil's condition prior to planting and implementing strategies for maintenance are essential for fostering robust plant growth. Soil structure, determined by particle size and pH levels (acidity or alkalinity), significantly influences plant selection and soil management practices.

pH levels are critical for plant nutrient uptake. Soils can range from acidic (pH 3.5) sphagnum moss peat to alkaline (pH 8.5) fine loam. Most herbs thrive in a fairly neutral pH range of 6.5 to 7.5. Alkaline soils can lead to stunted growth and nutrient deficiencies, while acidic soils may hinder certain plant varieties.

- **Clay Soil, pH 6.5**

Clay soil is dense, nutrient-rich, and prone to waterlogging in winter and dehydration in summer. Its fine particles cause soil compaction, making it challenging for roots to penetrate. While clay soil holds nutrients well, it benefits from the incorporation of well-rotted leaf mould or compost to enhance structure and facilitate plant establishment. Despite its challenges, with proper management, clay soil can yield rewarding results over time.

Understanding Different Soil Types

• Chalk Soil, pH 8.5
Comprised mainly of calcium carbonate, chalky soils lean towards alkalinity. Light in texture with occasional flint or chalk fragments, they boast good drainage but are often shallow. While compost can enrich nutrient content, adjusting pH levels to suit herb growth is challenging. Consider raised beds for easier cultivation.

• Loam Soil, pH 5.5–8.5
Loam, a gardener's delight, is a balanced blend of clay, sand, and silt, offering fertility, drainage, and workability. Various types exist, from clay-loam to sandy-loam, each with distinct characteristics suitable for herb cultivation. Sandy-loam, in particular, provides optimal conditions for a wide range of herbs due to its fertility and drainage.

- **Sand, pH 4.5**

Sandy soils are lightweight, warm, and low in nutrients, often tending towards acidity. Despite being easy to cultivate, they drain rapidly, leading to nutrient leaching and moisture loss. Winter feeding with leaf mould and well-rotted manure helps retain moisture and replenish nutrients. Early spring planting benefits from their quick warming properties.

Other soil types, such as silt and peat soils, offer varying degrees of fertility, moisture retention, and workability. Identifying your soil type involves tactile assessment: clay feels sticky when wet, chalk froths in vinegar, and sandy soil crumbles easily.

Understanding Soil pH

Soil pH, vital for nutrient absorption, can be determined using simple testing kits available at garden centers. Acidic soils turn yellow, neutral soils green, and alkaline soils dark green, indicating their respective pH levels.

Working with, Maintaining & Improving Soils

• **Clay Soils**

Rich in nutrients but prone to drainage issues, clay soils benefit from organic matter addition to enhance structure, warmth, and nutrient availability for plant roots.

• **Chalk Soils**

Highly alkaline, chalk soils pose challenges for acid-loving plants. Raised beds or container gardening are viable options for herb cultivation in these conditions.

• **Loam Soils**

Despite their balanced properties, loam soils require regular organic matter supplementation, especially with frequent cultivation.

- **Sandy Soils**

Low in nutrients and water-retentive capacity, sandy soils benefit from organic matter incorporation to improve fertility and moisture retention, reducing the need for frequent watering.

Chapter 5

How To Grow Herbs From Seed Successfully Every Time

Growing herbs from seed can be an enjoyable and fulfilling endeavor, offering the satisfaction of serving homegrown produce for dinner, alongside the health and environmental benefits of growing your own food.

To maximize your success, it's crucial to have some background knowledge and research the basics. Here are five essential tips for growing herbs from seed:

1. Determine whether you'll be growing your herbs indoors or outdoors, as this will influence the equipment you'll need.
2. Check historical climate data for your area to determine the typical last spring frost date.
3. Deduct 6-8 weeks from this date to know when to plant your herb seeds.
4. Ensure the growing medium allows sufficient space for root development over this period, such as using pots with a diameter of at least 2-3 inches.

Once you've decided when and where to start your herb garden, it's time to gather your supplies. While these materials are available at local hardware stores, it's recommended to opt for high-quality seeds and supplies tailored to your environment, especially if you're gardening in an urban setting. Essential supplies include:

- High-quality seeds, preferably compact with dense foliage and better pest and disease resistance.

- Seed starting mix, such as Rosy Soil, which is peat-free and contains worm castings.
- Coco coir pots, ideal for easy transplantation and backyard composting.

For indoor herb gardening, consider using self-watering ceramic planters, particularly for herbs like dill, parsley, and cilantro, which may not enjoy transplanting. These planters provide consistent hydration by slowly releasing water into the soil.

If time is of the essence, you may want to start with some of the fastest-growing herbs:

- Dill: Ready for harvest in about 40 days from sprouting.
- Cilantro: Leaves can be harvested after 50-60 days.
- Basil: Fresh basil leaves can be picked after 50-60 days.

Before setting up, consider soaking certain herb seeds like parsley and coriander for 12-24 hours to soften their hard outer shells and improve germination rates, although this step is not essential.

Determining the optimal temperature for herb growth is essential, as herbs are sensitive to temperature extremes. Both excessively hot and cold conditions can pose problems for their growth.

When starting seeds indoors, particularly in preparation for spring, cold windowsills present a significant threat. While sunlight becomes crucial after sprouting, during the germination stage, temperature holds greater importance. Herb seeds possess an innate sense to delay sprouting in cold conditions, perceiving it as winter. To simulate spring-like conditions, maintain temperatures between 65 - 75°F. If your indoor environment doesn't naturally accommodate this range, consider using a heat mat under the seeds during germination.

Certain herb seeds require light for germination and should be placed on or near the surface, while others prefer darkness and should be lightly covered with soil, typically to a depth no greater than the seed's length. Herbs that benefit from light for germination include thyme and lemon balm, whereas most others, such as basil, chives, cilantro, and others, prefer a slightly darker environment.

Planting distances vary depending on the herb species. For instance, oregano seeds, which germinate within 7-14 days, should be planted at least 18-22 inches apart.

Labeling your herb garden seeds is essential, even though it may seem obvious. Seedlings are challenging to differentiate, making it crucial to use stickers or labels to mark each variety.

Transplanting herbs from indoor containers to outdoor gardens is a straightforward process, providing flexibility in managing your herb garden.

Chapter 6

Providing Adequate Water

Ensuring adequate water supply is crucial for nurturing various herbs, offering not only environmental benefits but also serving as a simple and enjoyable introduction to gardening, especially for beginners.

Herbs, although generally low-maintenance, possess distinct watering requirements essential for their thriving. Here are seven watering guidelines tailored to herb cultivation:

1. Avoid Houseplant Watering Methods:

- Herbs differ from houseplants in their watering needs. Unlike houseplants, herbs dislike standing water or overly moist soil. Water herbs only when the soil feels dry to the touch, particularly crucial for herbs grown from seed or within herb garden kits to prevent seedling drowning.

2. Watering Moisture-Loving Herbs:

- Moisture-loving herbs require approximately ½ liter of water per square foot of soil weekly when planted in the ground. For potted herbs, watering once or twice daily is advisable, especially during summer, but always assess soil moisture before watering.

3. Indoor Herb Watering Regimen:

- Indoor herbs typically necessitate watering every two to three days. Verify soil moisture by feeling the top inch of soil. Dryness at this depth indicates a need for watering. Outdoor herbs should be watered daily under normal conditions and twice daily during hot weather or dry seasons.

4. Optimal Watering Time:

- The ideal time to water herbs is in the morning around 6 to 6:30 AM when the sun is rising. This timing ensures maximum moisture absorption by the roots before water evaporation due to heat, especially crucial for herbs from garden kits or starter plants.

5. Targeted Watering Technique:

- Watering around the herb's base, avoiding wetting the leaves, is imperative. Moist leaves elevate the risk of mold, mildew, and rot, potentially harming the herb's health.

6. Consider Bottom Watering:

- Some pots feature built-in saucers or reservoirs to maintain root hydration. For such pots, allow the roots to soak for a maximum of 15 minutes to prevent waterlogging. Discard excess water to mitigate the risk of root rot and disease.

Mulching

Using mulch is a common practice to conserve soil moisture, reducing the frequency of watering required. When applied to an in-ground herb garden, mulch not only serves a functional purpose but also enhances its visual appeal. However, it's crucial to select mulching materials that are safe for herbs. Natural options like wood chips, cocoa bean shells, or pine needles are preferable. Ensure the mulch layer is kept away from the herb's crown to prevent suffocation of the plant.

Identifying signs of overwatering is essential for maintaining healthy herbs and vegetables in the garden. While most herbs thrive in moist conditions and full sunlight, improper watering techniques can lead to detrimental consequences. Here are indicators that you might be overwatering your herbs:

- Yellowing leaves
- Presence of fuzzy mildew on stems and leaves
- Stunted growth of herbs
- Lack of response from herbs when watered
- Fragile stems prone to breakage
- Abnormally soft roots
- Excessive leaf shedding

For those interested in building an herb garden, starting from seed offers a rewarding experience. Our herb garden kits provide all the necessary tools to establish a vibrant herb garden, making them ideal gifts as well!

Chapter 7

Fertilizing the Herbs

Fertilizing herbs is essential for their optimal growth, but not all herbs have the same fertilizer requirements. Understanding when and how much to fertilize depends on various factors such as the herb type, growing conditions, soil texture, and fertility.

Differentiating between slow-growing herbs native to the Mediterranean, characterized by small leaves and woody stems, and fast-growing herbs with larger, thinner leaves, is crucial. Slow-growers like bay laurel, lavender, mint, and thyme generally require less fertilizer compared to fast-growing counterparts such as basil, cilantro, and parsley.

For optimal growth, herbs benefit from planting in nutrient-rich soil supplemented with organic matter. A balanced, slow-release fertilizer containing equal parts of nitrogen, phosphorus, and potassium is recommended, especially for herbs grown in sandy soil where nutrients deplete quickly.

Fast-growing herbs, particularly those harvested frequently, may benefit from additional nitrogen-rich organic fertilizers like fish emulsion. However, over-fertilization should be avoided, and any yellowing of leaves should be carefully assessed before applying fertilizer.

In container gardening, herbs need more frequent fertilization due to rapid nutrient depletion from frequent watering. Slow-release fertilizers are preferred to prevent over-fertilization, and organic options are recommended to avoid salt buildup. Using a diluted strength of fertilizer as per label instructions helps prevent nutrient imbalances in container-grown herbs.

Fertilizing hydroponic herbs requires a different approach compared to those grown in traditional soil or potting mix. Hydroponic herbs need frequent fertilization, typically every two weeks or as directed by the hydroponic system's instructions, using specialized hydroponic fertilizer designed for vegetables and herbs.

Hydroponically grown basil, in particular, is prone to magnesium deficiency due to insufficient magnesium supply from the water or added fertilizer. This deficiency often presents as chlorotic yellowing between leaf veins. Addressing this issue involves adding a liquid magnesium supplement, commonly available as a calcium and magnesium combination, following the label instructions.

Over-fertilizing herbs can result in nitrogen excess, primarily affecting slow-growing varieties negatively. While nitrogen-induced rapid leaf growth benefits thin-leaved herbs like basil, it can diminish the aromatic concentration of essential oils in Mediterranean herbs like rosemary, leading to weaker flavor and aroma.

Fertilizing hydroponic herbs requires a different approach compared to those grown in traditional soil or potting mix. Hydroponic herbs need frequent fertilization, typically every two weeks or as directed by the hydroponic system's instructions, using specialized hydroponic fertilizer designed for vegetables and herbs.

Hydroponically grown basil, in particular, is prone to magnesium deficiency due to insufficient magnesium supply from the water or added fertilizer. This deficiency often presents as chlorotic yellowing between leaf veins. Addressing this issue involves adding a liquid magnesium supplement, commonly available as a calcium and magnesium combination, following the label instructions.

Over-fertilizing herbs can result in nitrogen excess, primarily affecting slow-growing varieties negatively. While nitrogen-induced rapid leaf growth benefits thin-leaved herbs like basil, it can diminish the aromatic concentration of essential oils in Mediterranean herbs like rosemary, leading to weaker flavor and aroma.

Chapter 8

HOW TO PRUNE HERBS FOR THE BEST AND FRESHEST RESULTS

To optimize the lushness and abundance of your herb garden, mastering the art of pruning is essential. Pruning involves selectively removing leaves and stems from your plants to encourage ongoing growth, ultimately shaping the garden's appearance and size. Here are key insights into effectively pruning your herbs:

Basic Principles:

Early and frequent pruning is advantageous for most plants, ideally starting when they are in their early stages of growth. This regular maintenance promotes optimal growth, shape, and enables early detection of any pest or disease issues.

Never exceed pruning more than one-third of the plant at any given time to avoid stunting its growth.

Cease pruning at least eight weeks before the onset of winter frost to allow new growth to fortify before colder weather arrives, a process known as "hardening off."

Understanding Herb Types:

Herbs can be broadly categorized as herbaceous or evergreen, each requiring distinct pruning approaches.

Herbaceous herbs, such as oregano and mint, typically wither in winter and do not necessitate precise pruning measures. Harvesting or removing blossoms serves as a sufficient pruning method.

Evergreen herbs like rosemary and sage benefit from annual pruning, either in early spring or fall, to maintain their shape and vitality.

Pruning Techniques:

Utilize fingers to pinch off leaves and stems for delicate plants, while scissors are suitable for others. Precision and cleanliness are essential to avoid tearing or damaging the plant.

Leafier plants like basil require regular pruning to prevent quick deterioration post-blossoming. Cut at the juncture where the leaf meets the stem.

For woodier herbs like rosemary and thyme, periodic trimming prevents excessive woodiness, stimulating new leaf growth. Pinch back leaves as soon as new growth emerges.

Strategic Approach:

Commence pruning from the top rather than the bottom to maintain a sturdy base. For instance, with basil, remove the newest leaves at the top while preserving the larger, lower leaves as the foundation.

Employ the "tipping" technique by trimming the top 1-2 inches of the stem to promote branching and bushier growth, enhancing foliage density.

With diligent pruning following these guidelines, your herb garden will flourish abundantly, yielding a bountiful harvest. While an Urban Cultivator unit streamlines much of the process, incorporating pruning ensures optimal crop development.

Chapter 9

How to Harvest Herbs so That the Leaves Keep on Coming

In the journey of learning gardening, herbs are placed prominently for good reasons: they demand minimal care and gardening expertise to thrive. When cultivated in suitable conditions, herbs exhibit remarkable generosity, continuously yielding delicious leaves with each harvest.

Regular harvesting stands as the primary care task for herbs, offering benefits beyond just culinary delight. Besides enhancing your meals, picking leaves serves as a natural defense against pests, wards off diseases, and stimulates ongoing leaf production.

Harvesting techniques vary based on the herb type, which conveniently falls into two categories:

1. Annual herbs, also termed "soft herbs," are sown from seed each year. Popular examples include cilantro, dill, parsley, and basil.
2. Perennial herbs, known as "woody herbs," either persist throughout the year in mild climates or regenerate from their roots in colder regions. Notable perennials encompass rosemary, sage, oregano, mint, and thyme.

Regardless of the herb variety, adhering to three fundamental rules of herb harvesting is crucial.

Adhere to these three guidelines while harvesting herbs from your garden to ensure abundant leaf yields in the future.

RULE 1: USE SANITIZED TOOLS

Employ clean needle nose pruners, sharp scissors, or garden snips to harvest your herbs. Prior to each harvest session, sanitize your cutting tools with rubbing alcohol. This precautionary measure minimizes the risk of transmitting any potential pathogens like diseases or fungi to your precious herb plants.

RULE 2: HARVEST DRY LEAVES

Ensure that your herbs are dry before harvesting. If they've been exposed to rain or irrigation, wait until the foliage has thoroughly dried. Harvesting from damp plants increases susceptibility to mold or mildew, and it diminishes the shelf life of your harvested leaves. Ideally, harvest early in the day, after the morning dew has evaporated, to preserve maximum flavor and longevity.

RULE 3: ADHERE TO THE GOLDEN RULE

Adhere to the Golden Rule of Harvesting, limiting your harvest to no more than one-third of any individual herb within a given week. This practice allows plants ample time to recover and continue photosynthesizing, ensuring sustained productivity and future harvests.

When to Harvest Annual Herbs

Annual herbs such as parsley, cilantro, and dill typically require 45 to 60 days from seed to maturity in the garden. It's best to wait until these soft-leaved herbs have developed at least 5 to 10 main stems before your initial harvest. Cilantro and dill generally last around 90 to 120 days, while parsley can potentially persist for up to two years, being technically a biennial.

Basil can be harvested once the plant has produced a couple of sets of leaves.

Given that annual herbs tend to bolt in unfavorable temperatures, it's crucial to harvest frequently and replant continuously to ensure a steady supply of leaves throughout the year. Aim to harvest one to three stems per week from each annual plant during its peak growing season, as frequent harvesting stimulates further growth.

Here's how to harvest your annual herbs effectively, ensuring a bountiful yield and prolonged enjoyment:

Harvesting Cilantro, Dill, & Parsley:
Similar to harvesting lettuces and leafy greens, harvesting soft herbs like cilantro, dill, and parsley involves cutting from the outer portions of the plant. If you notice tall center stalks emerging, it's a sign of bolting, usually due to temperature changes. Trim these tall stems to prolong leaf harvests.

When harvesting these herbs, cut down to the base of the stem rather than just snipping the leaves, as the stems won't regenerate from the tips. Leave the smaller leaves at the center to continue growing. After cutting, immediately place the stems in a jar of water to prevent wilting. They can be stored in the fridge this way for a couple of days.

Harvesting Basil:
For basil, focus on encouraging a bushy growth pattern rather than tall flowering spikes. Instead of cutting from the sides, target the top of the plant. Cut just above a leaf node to stimulate branching out of the stems.

After harvesting basil, treat it like fresh-cut flowers. Place the sprigs in water and display them on your countertop at room temperature for optimal enjoyment.

Savoring Your Annual Herbs:
Freshness is key when it comes to enjoying annual herbs, as they tend to lose their flavor rapidly.

Cilantro adds a vibrant touch to dishes like tacos and salads.

Dill infuses meals with a zesty, slightly citrusy flavor, perfect for dips, potato salad, or dill pesto.

Parsley complements salads, tabbouleh, and chimichurri, and serves as a garnish for soups, stews, and cooked fish. Consider substituting a dash of parsley for salt in recipes to enhance flavor.

Since these herbs don't dry well, preserve them by blending with oil and freezing in an ice cube tray for later use. Alternatively, freeze them whole.

Pro tip: Store each herb separately to maintain its distinct flavor profile.

Enjoying Basil:
Basil offers versatility in culinary delights. Whether you're crafting a caprese salad, enhancing pizza toppings, or whipping up a batch of pesto, fresh basil leaves add vibrant flavor to your dishes. For a delightful twist, try making an herb garden flatbread

featuring freshly harvested basil alongside oregano for an easy family favorite.

While basil doesn't dry as well as some other herbs, it fares better than most annual herbs when dried, providing a taste of summer throughout the winter months. Alternatively, you can freeze chopped basil leaves in oil for longer preservation.

Harvesting Perennial Herbs:
The timing of your perennial herb harvest depends on their source and growth rate. For herbs started from seeds, wait at least 30 to 45 days before the first harvest. Nursery-bought plants allow immediate cutting but ease into it, waiting a month or two before more extensive harvesting. Cuttings take about four to six weeks to establish before harvesting.

Weekly or even daily harvesting of established perennial herbs like sage, rosemary, mint, thyme, and oregano encourages continuous leaf growth.

Aim to cut 3 to 4 stems per week during peak seasons to promote abundant growth.

When harvesting, begin from the outermost branches, pinching back just above a leaf node to encourage branching. For spreading herbs like mint, thyme, and oregano, thin out by cutting long stems to the base to promote vine-like growth.

Enjoying Perennial Herbs:
Perennial herb leaves can be enjoyed fresh or dried for later use. To dry, strip bottom leaves, tie bunches, and hang upside down in a dry, shaded area until brittle. Store dried leaves in glass jars for year-round use.

Keep sage, rosemary, oregano, and thyme fresh in the fridge for up to a week by wrapping in a paper towel and storing in a bag or container. Mint stems are best kept fresh by placing in water on the countertop.

Sage Delights:

Savor sage by pinching off individual leaves or harvesting entire sprigs. Add sage to browned butter for pasta dishes, pair with butternut squash, or complement chicken and pork for a flavorful culinary experience.

Enjoying Rosemary:

Embrace the aromatic richness of dried rosemary in your culinary creations, whether it's soups, stews, or roasted dishes, particularly those featuring chicken.

Savoring Mint:

Fresh mint adds a burst of freshness to Mediterranean-style dishes like couscous paired with feta and roasted tomatoes.

Dried mint, whether peppermint or spearmint, is a delightful addition to your pantry, perfect for crafting soothing mint tea.

Indulging in Thyme:

Both fresh and dried thyme complement roasted vegetables, meats, soups, and various dishes with their robust flavor.

Delighting in Oregano:

Fresh oregano enhances the flavors of homemade pizzas, spaghetti sauce, and tacos, lending them a savory note.

Dried oregano is ideal for blending into salt mixtures or creating all-purpose seasoning blends alongside other dried herbs from your garden.

Harvesting Chives:

Chives, known for their prolific growth and flavorful contribution to meals, require a distinct harvesting method. Begin harvesting approximately 60 days after planting from seed, allowing transplants several weeks to acclimate.

To harvest chives, gather multiple stems and trim them low, about 1 to 2 inches above the soil, using clean scissors or snips. New growth emerges from the plant center, emphasizing the importance of regular pruning to maintain health and productivity.

Chives add a delightful garlicky or oniony essence to dishes like omelets, roasted veggies, and cooked meats.

Final Thoughts on Herb Harvesting:
By adopting these harvesting techniques, you can cultivate a bountiful supply of herbs, reducing reliance on store-bought options. Regular pruning and strategic harvest storage can ensure a year-round abundance, with plenty to share among neighbors and friends—a gift cherished for its homegrown essence.

Chapter 10

Protecting from Pests and Diseases

Maintaining healthy herbs is straightforward if you adhere to several fundamental guidelines. Most herbs thrive in sunny locations, necessitating a minimum of six hours of sunlight daily. Additionally, well-drained soil with a pH level ranging from 6 to 7, enriched with organic compost, is favored by herbs. Regular pruning, which involves eliminating weak or infected growth, is crucial for protecting herbs from pests and diseases. However, certain common pests and diseases may still affect herb gardens.

Shielding Herbs from Pests

The aromatic oils inherent in most herbs naturally repel numerous insects. Nevertheless, occasional pests like slugs can infiltrate herb gardens and cause damage. Fortunately, most of these pests are merely bothersome and seldom inflict severe harm. Aphids, spider mites, whiteflies, leafhoppers, and leaf miners are some common pests that may affect herbs. Various measures, including horticultural soaps and neem oil, can help eliminate these pests effectively.

Diseases Affecting Herbs

Few herbs, notably mints and lemongrass, thrive in wet soil conditions, which can foster fungal diseases like fusarium root rot. Rust is another common disease affecting herbs, characterized by rusty orange lesions on leaf undersides. Combatting herb diseases involves providing optimal growing conditions, maintaining sanitation, removing weak or infested foliage, and regular pruning. Raised beds promote adequate drainage, while morning watering aids in minimizing the spread of fungal spores.

Troubleshooting Herb Gardens

When troubleshooting herb gardens, adhering to the following golden rules is essential:

1. Select healthy herbs for planting and ensure they are suited to their environment.
2. Avoid overcrowding, allowing ample space for growth and airflow.
3. Practice appropriate irrigation and fertilization, preferably with organic options like compost tea.
4. Regularly prune herbs to encourage healthy growth and remove diseased foliage.

Adhering to these guidelines minimizes the need for chemical controls in herb gardens, promoting healthier and safer herb cultivation practices.

Chapter 11

Culinary Herbs

1. Anise

Anise, often overlooked in herb gardens, deserves a place among your plants due to its Mediterranean origin and licorice-like aroma. Its robust nature makes it suitable for use in curries, flavored liqueurs, and baking, with its seeds being the edible part. Anise thrives best in warm seasons and is an annual herb, requiring replanting each year.

Planting Instructions:
Anise is easily grown by direct sowing into garden beds with well-draining, weed-free soil, and a temperature of at least 60 degrees Fahrenheit. Plant

seeds half an inch deep, spaced one inch apart, with rows set two to three feet apart.

Growing Tips:

Anise prefers alkaline soil with a pH between 6.3 and 7.0, full sun exposure, and regular watering until established, after which it can withstand dry periods. Container gardening is also an option for those with limited outdoor space.

Harvesting:

Anise seeds are not only useful in cooking but also possess medicinal properties, aiding digestion and respiratory illnesses. Crushed seeds emit a pleasant aroma and can be added to various products like soaps and perfumes. Harvesting occurs approximately 120 days after planting, with leaves and seeds being usable in both fresh and dried forms.

Fertilization:

While herbs generally don't require fertilization, anise benefits from a nitrogen-heavy fertilizer before flowering, supplemented with compost before planting.

2. Basil

Basil, an adaptable annual herb, enhances various culinary dishes, including pasta sauces, salads, and Thai curries. Belonging to the mint family, basil can be grown by sowing seeds successively from spring to summer, followed by potting into individual containers. Proper watering and regular harvesting using scissors or snips promote bushier and more productive plants.

Growing Instructions:
Start basil seedlings in moist seed compost or quality multi-purpose compost in a warm, bright environment. Pot seedlings into individual containers once large enough, and gradually acclimate them to outdoor conditions before transplanting.

Care Tips:
Avoid overwatering basil, as excessive moisture may lead to wilting and root rot. Provide protection

from wind and cold air, and avoid wetting the leaves to prevent fungal growth. Expect rapid growth in containers, necessitating repotting during the growing season.

Harvesting and Usage:
Regularly harvest basil leaves throughout summer, leaving side shoots intact for regrowth. Use fresh basil in salads, pesto, sauces, and curries, adding it towards the end of cooking for optimal flavor. Fresh storage is preferable, though cut stems can be kept in water for a few days.

Seed Availability:
Basil seeds are widely available from online retailers, garden centers, and local shops, offering a diverse range of varieties for cultivation from seed, allowing for broader selection and potential seedling exchanges among gardeners.

3. Bay

Bay, scientifically known as Laurus nobilis, is an aromatic evergreen shrub appreciated for its fragrant leaves. Introduced to British gardens in 1650, bay leaves hold a crucial place in herb gardens, lending their flavor to an array of dishes such as soups, stews, and even ice cream. Whether used fresh or dried, bay leaves are prized for their culinary contributions. This slow-growing shrub can take several years to reach a height of up to 8 meters and is often shaped into topiary forms, adding elegance to garden landscapes.

Growing Requirements:
Bay thrives in fertile, well-drained soil and prefers full sun, ideally positioned near a south- or west-facing wall. In cooler climates, it can be cultivated in pots, offering the flexibility to move indoors during autumn. Pruning during summer and rejuvenating older plants in spring are essential for maintaining healthy growth. Bay leaves can be

harvested year-round, ready for immediate use or dried for future storage.

Cultivation Tips:

Native to the Mediterranean, bay trees flourish in sunny to partially shaded areas with protection from harsh elements, tolerating temperatures as low as -5°C. Planting directly into the ground allows for the establishment of a robust root system, while potted specimens require regular watering and drainage to prevent waterlogging. Periodic feeding with a liquid fertilizer during the growing season promotes healthy growth.

Propagation and Maintenance:

Propagating bay involves taking semi-ripe cuttings in late summer or layering in spring. Pruning is crucial for shaping and rejuvenating plants, particularly in late spring and summer. Vigilance against pests like bay leaf suckers is necessary, with prompt removal of affected leaves to prevent infestation.

Considerations and Remedies:

Bay trees are valued investments, available in various forms at garden centers. While resilient, they may suffer damage from harsh winters, necessitating careful assessment and potential repotting. Concerns regarding subsidence near houses, particularly those with clay soil, should be addressed by monitoring root growth and pruning when necessary. Pest management, such as addressing bay tree suckers, involves careful observation and potential intervention to maintain plant health without harming beneficial predators.

In conclusion, bay trees offer not only culinary delights but also ornamental beauty, making them a prized addition to any garden landscape.

4. Borage

Borage, also recognized as bugloss or starflower (Borago officinalis), is an annual flowering herb originating from Mediterranean regions. Characterized by its spreading bushy plants reaching 60cm in height, borage boasts star-shaped pure blue flowers from early summer to autumn, attracting bees with its nectar-rich blooms. Beyond its ornamental appeal, borage serves as an edible herb, with its blossoms commonly used to garnish summer drinks like Pimms, while its young leaves offer a refreshing cucumber-like flavor ideal for salads and dressings.

Cultivation Tips:

Thriving in sunny locations with well-drained soil, borage proves beneficial when grown alongside fruits and vegetables, attracting pollinators to enhance crop yields. Despite its late blooming cycle, which extends until the first frosts, caution is advised when handling borage due to its hairy leaves, which may cause skin irritation in sensitive individuals.

Planting and Maintenance:

Easily grown from seed directly in the ground, borage requires minimal maintenance, making it an ideal choice for filling gaps in flower borders or as part of an annual flower display. Optimal growth conditions include a well-drained, sun-drenched site, with no additional fertilization necessary, as borage thrives in low-fertility soil.

Versatility and Varieties:

With various applications ranging from culinary to medicinal, borage offers versatility in both its uses and growth habits. While Borago officinalis is the most common variety, distinguished by its star-shaped blue flowers, alternatives like Borago officinalis 'Alba' with white blooms, and the low-growing Borago pygmaea provide additional options for gardeners.

5. Caraway

Caraway, prized for its aromatic seeds, serves as a flavorful addition to a wide range of culinary delights, including baking, soups, and stews. As a biennial plant, caraway requires patience, typically spending its first season establishing vegetative growth before setting seed in its second year.

Growing Requirements:

Native to Europe and western Asia, caraway thrives in full sun and well-drained soil with a pH range of 6.5 to 7.0, preferring cool temperate climates over hot, humid conditions. Sowing seeds directly in fall or spring facilitates germination, with subsequent thinning to 8 to 12 inches apart promoting optimal growth.

Cultivation and Harvesting:

While minimal cultivation is needed, ensuring adequate moisture during the first year is crucial for optimal development. Harvesting occurs once the seeds turn a rich, deep brown color, typically achieved by cutting the umbels from the plant and allowing them to dry before extracting the flavorful spice. With all parts of the plant being edible, caraway offers a versatile addition to herb gardens, enriching both culinary creations and spice racks alike.

6. Chamomile

Chamomile, a resilient perennial adorned with delicate, aromatic leaves and charming white daisy-like blooms, boasts an impressive array of medicinal properties, including anti-allergy, anti-inflammatory, and calming effects. Its rich historical usage dates back to ancient Egypt, where evidence suggests it was employed for both healing ailments and preservation rituals. Today, chamomile remains popular primarily for its soothing tea, readily available in dried form within supermarket tea bags.

Species and Cultivation:

The two most cultivated species for chamomile tea production are German chamomile (Matricaria recutita) and Roman chamomile (Chamaemelum nobile), both thriving in similar growing conditions. Requiring well-drained soil and either full sun or partial shade, these species exhibit drought tolerance once established, necessitating watering only during prolonged dry spells.

Growing Techniques:

Chamomile cultivation typically involves direct sowing in prepared seedbeds during autumn or indoor sowing from March onwards. Seeds are evenly scattered over moist, peat-free compost, optionally covered with a thin layer of vermiculite. Indoor-grown seedlings are potted individually and gradually acclimatized before transplanting outdoors post-frost.

Maintenance and Harvesting:

Once established, chamomile demands minimal upkeep, displaying resilience to drought conditions. Regular watering is advised for potted plants, ensuring proper drainage to prevent waterlogging. Pruning aids in maintaining compact growth and averting legginess. Harvesting chamomile flowers can be done as needed, with excess blooms dried for future use in a warm, dry area away from direct sunlight.

Utilization and Sources:

Chamomile flowers, whether fresh or dried, serve as the foundation for brewing soothing teas renowned for aiding digestion and promoting relaxation. When purchasing chamomile, discern between German and Roman varieties, considering their differing heights. Adhering to seed packet instructions and inspecting pot-grown plants for pest or disease signs ensures successful cultivation. Sources like Gardeners' World offer chamomile seeds for purchase, facilitating home cultivation for interested gardeners.

In essence, chamomile stands as a versatile perennial herb, celebrated for its medicinal virtues and cherished as a staple in tea culture. Cultivating chamomile entails straightforward procedures, making it accessible for both novice and seasoned gardeners seeking to incorporate this botanical gem into their green spaces.

7. Chervil

Chervil (Anthriscus cerefolium), an edible herb prized for its finely divided verdant leaves, is renowned in culinary circles for its subtle and delicate flavor profile. It features prominently in the classic French herb blend known as 'fines herbes,' alongside parsley, tarragon, and chives, adding a distinctive touch to various dishes. Despite its culinary prowess, chervil is straightforward to cultivate, thriving without the need for specialized growing conditions. The superiority of fresh chervil over its dried counterpart is a hallmark of its culinary appeal.

Often dubbed French parsley, chervil bears a resemblance in appearance and taste to parsley (Petroselinum crispum), despite lacking botanical kinship. Additionally, it bears no relation to chervil root (Chaerophyllum bulbosum), a root vegetable resembling parsnip. Originating from the Middle East and Caucasus regions, chervil likely found its way to Britain during Roman times and has since been cultivated for centuries. Its hardiness renders it a valuable asset, offering fresh harvests even during the winter months when culinary herbs are scarce.

Cultivation:

To cultivate chervil, sow seeds from spring through late summer in a cool, partially shaded location directly in the desired growing area. Thinning seedlings and ensuring adequate hydration during dry spells are essential practices. Harvesting can commence when plants reach a few weeks of age, discarding specimens prone to bolting and removing faded flower heads to prevent self-seeding.

Growing Conditions:

Chervil thrives in partial shade, benefiting from protection against the midday sun during the summer to prevent premature bolting. Its aesthetic appeal makes it a suitable companion for ornamental plants in garden borders or as a complement to vegetables in the garden. While ground cultivation is optimal, chervil adapts well to large containers.

Care and Harvesting:
Proper care involves diligent watering, prompt removal of flower stems, and protection with cloches in colder regions. Allowing some flowers to set seed enables natural propagation or the collection of seeds for future planting. Harvesting entails picking fully unfurled leaves around six to eight weeks post-sowing, avoiding specimens with flowering stems, which develop a bitter taste. Storing chopped leaves in ice cube trays submerged in water before freezing ensures a readily accessible supply.

Utilization and Pest Management:
Chervil's delicate flavor complements a wide array of dishes, particularly those featuring mild-tasting ingredients like eggs, white fish, and poultry, while also lending itself to soups, stews, and vegetable preparations. Employing chervil in herb-infused

butter and oil adds a fresh touch to culinary creations, best added towards the end of cooking to preserve its flavor. Vigilant pest management, utilizing eco-friendly barriers or baits, is advisable, especially during the vulnerable seedling stage. Procuring seeds from reputable sources or verifying freshness ensures optimal germination rates for consistent yields.

In essence, chervil stands as a versatile culinary herb prized for its subtle yet distinctive flavor and ease of cultivation. Its presence in the garden not only enhances culinary endeavors but also adds aesthetic charm, making it a valuable addition to any herbaceous repertoire.

8. Chives

Chives, renowned for their versatility and ease of cultivation, thrive in diverse climates, from hot to cold regions. This herbaceous perennial encompasses two main types: garlic chives and onion chives (common chives), each characterized by distinct leaf structures and heights. While garlic chives boast flat leaves and can reach heights of up to 20 inches, onion chives feature slender, hollow leaves and typically grow between 10 to 15 inches tall.

Distinguished by their robust garlic flavor, chives are both edible and attractive to pollinators. Despite their association with the onion family, they differ from green onions, which exhibit thicker stems transitioning from green tops to firm white bases, and offer a milder taste compared to their counterparts.

Cold-hardy perennials by nature, chives reemerge annually from their root systems, adapting well to various climatic conditions. In zones 9 and 10, chives may thrive year-round with adequate watering during hot spells. Conversely, in colder locales, they undergo seasonal dieback after frost or snowfall, resurging with the onset of spring. Their propagation occurs via dropped seeds and subterranean bulbs.

Ideal for placement in raised bed corners or along container garden perimeters, chives serve as natural pest repellents, deterring undesirable insects with their pungent onion or garlic aroma. For container cultivation, opt for vessels with a depth of at least 6 inches and ensure proper drainage to prevent waterlogging.

While partial shade is tolerated, chives prefer full sun, albeit benefitting from afternoon shade during scorching summers.

Summary:

Chives represent a versatile and uncomplicated addition to any garden, thriving in varied climates with minimal care requirements. Cultivating your own organic chives ensures a readily accessible source of this flavorful herb, enriching culinary creations and supporting pollinator populations.

Kickstarting chive cultivation can occur indoors approximately 6 to 8 weeks before the final frost of spring or through direct sowing in garden beds post-soil preparation. Alternatively, nursery-acquired chive plants offer a convenient shortcut to expedited harvests and year-round growth. In warmer regions, fall planting is viable, provided plants receive ample time to establish before the initial frost.

To initiate chive growth from seeds, adhere to the following steps:

1. Prepare the soil by clearing debris and enriching it with fresh compost.
2. Sow seeds by gently pressing them into the soil surface.
3. Water gently to avoid seed displacement.
4. Optimize growth conditions with consistent moisture levels and ample illumination, employing grow lights if necessary.

Chive maintenance entails providing 6+ hours of sunlight to encourage flowering, ensuring optimal growth. While chives will endure with as little as 4 to 6 hours of daily sunlight, their growth rate may diminish, and flowering may be less prolific.

Sustaining healthy chive growth relies on nutrient-rich soil, obviating the need for fertilization with periodic additions of fresh compost or worm castings. Consistent watering, particularly for potted specimens, prevents soil desiccation and promotes robust growth.

Chives serve as invaluable companions in kitchen gardens, warding off pests and attracting pollinators to neighboring vegetables and herbs. Their compatibility with perennial mint family herbs, such as rosemary, sage, thyme, oregano, and lavender, underscores their versatility in garden planning.

In conclusion, chives offer a rewarding and straightforward cultivation experience, yielding an abundant harvest within 60 days of seeding or upon maturity of nursery-acquired plants. Employing proper harvesting techniques ensures sustained productivity, enabling continual utilization in various culinary endeavors. From savory dishes to floral garnishes, chives impart their unique flavor profile, enriching culinary creations and elevating dining experiences.

9. Cilantro/Coriander

Cilantro, a versatile addition to any kitchen garden, yields flavorful seeds known as coriander, enhancing various culinary creations. To preserve coriander seeds from your cilantro plants, adhere to these straightforward guidelines:

1. Allow cilantro plants to reach the seeding stage. As cilantro bolts, it produces delicate white or pale pink flowers, facilitating pollination. These flowers give rise to green pods harboring developing coriander seeds. These seeds can be consumed while green, imparting a mildly spicy flavor, or dried for future use.

2. Harvest cilantro plants. Remove the entire plant by cutting it at the base, leaving the roots intact to avoid disturbing neighboring plants. Consider replanting cilantro for a continuous supply of fresh leaves.

3. Dry cilantro. Bundle cilantro stems and suspend them upside down in a cool, dark, and dry environment until fully dried, ensuring no greenness remains on the stems.

4. Separate coriander seeds from the pods. Coriander seeds are ready when they turn light brown with visible ridges. Rinse the seeds in a kitchen strainer, removing any residual pod remnants while minimizing seed damage.

5. Store coriander seeds. If intending to sow the seeds, allow them to rest for a brief period before planting. Utilize seeds from a fresh packet if planning immediate sowing. A single harvest from three cilantro plants typically yields approximately 500 coriander seeds, ensuring an ample supply for various culinary endeavors.

Enhance your gardening experience with our Preferred Seed Organizer. This convenient tin keeps seeds meticulously organized, ensuring they're readily available for planting at optimal times. Its galvanized finish offers timeless appeal, while calendar dividers facilitate precise seed management for optimal planting schedules.

Coriander holds a prominent place in spice blends like garam masala and Indian curries, and it finds applications in pickling recipes. Our comprehensive set includes essential tools such as a mini dibber for effortless herb planting, mini pruners to maintain garden tidiness, specialized herb scissors for efficient harvesting, and charming wooden plant labels for herb identification. Additionally, our herb drying rack facilitates the preservation of herbs for winter use.

In conclusion, cultivating and harvesting coriander seeds from cilantro plants presents a simple yet rewarding endeavor. By following these steps, you can enjoy the satisfaction of producing your own coriander seeds and relish their delectable contributions to your culinary creations.

10. Cumin

Cumin, scientifically known as Cuminum cyminum, is an annual flowering plant belonging to the parsley family, Apiaceae, valued for its aromatic seeds. Widely utilized across diverse cuisines, it stands as one of the most sought-after spices globally, boasting warm, earthy undertones with a hint of bitterness, lending itself well to a myriad of culinary creations. Particularly prominent in Indian, Mediterranean, Middle Eastern, North African, and Mexican cuisines, its versatility knows no bounds.

Reaching heights of 1 to 2 feet, cumin produces clusters of fragrant pink or white flowers amidst foliage resembling that of dill, typically emerging in midsummer. These flowers precede the development of the characteristic aromatic seeds, which mature approximately 120 days after planting. Beyond their culinary value, cumin flowers serve as a beacon for beneficial insects like lacewings, predatory wasps, and ladybugs, aiding in natural pest control when strategically positioned within the garden.

Originating from the eastern Mediterranean, parts of the Middle East, and India, cumin boasts a rich historical lineage, revered both as a culinary staple and a medicinal aid. Ancient Egyptians integrated its seeds into their cuisine and mummification rituals, while ancient Greeks echoed modern practices by incorporating it into table-side condiments akin to contemporary black pepper usage.

Notably, cuminaldehyde, a volatile oil found within cumin seeds, flaunts anti-inflammatory, antioxidant, and carminative properties, underpinning its medicinal appeal. Its therapeutic legacy endures in practices like Ayurveda, where it finds application in alleviating digestive discomfort, bloating, and facilitating fat assimilation.

Cultivating cumin demands a frost-free environment and an extended hot growing season. In regions subject to colder climates, indoor seed starting becomes imperative, with seedlings transplanted post-last frost date, ideally when temperatures consistently surpass 60°F. Employing biodegradable pots or soil blocks for seedling propagation circumvents transplant shock and promotes seamless growth transitions.

In warmer climes with frost-free intervals spanning at least four months, direct outdoor sowing emerges as the preferred method. Seed placement in well-drained, sun-soaked soil, spaced 4 to 8 inches apart, ensures optimal growth conditions, with germination typically occurring within 14 days. However, it's prudent to allocate a substantial growing area, considering each plant's modest seed yield.

Thriving within USDA Hardiness Zones 5-10, cumin thrives in nutrient-rich sandy loam soils, demonstrating resilience against drought conditions while necessitating periodic watering during prolonged dry spells. Misting routines and mulching practices serve to regulate soil moisture levels, ensuring optimal plant health and productivity.

To encapsulate, cumin's significance transcends mere culinary prowess, offering a fusion of flavor and therapeutic utility. Whether in the kitchen or the garden, its presence enriches both the palate and the landscape, underscoring its indispensable role in the realm of herbs and spices.

Chapter 12

Medicinal Herbs

1. Angelica

Angelica, a tall biennial herb featuring expansive, domed flower clusters and delicate seed pods, serves as a favored selection for wildlife-friendly gardens, owing to its charming blooms and edible seeds. With highly aromatic components, various parts of the plant have found utility in both medicinal and culinary domains. Thriving in partially shaded, moisture-rich soil, angelica can be cultivated either through module planting or direct sowing into the ground.

The process of planting angelica entails seeding during autumn or late spring, followed by stem pruning and plant extraction come the autumn of its second year. Subsequent to root division using a sharp blade, the segments are repotted into compost or the designated soil plot. For the creation of candied angelica, tender young stems are harvested in spring before June.

In terms of storage, preparation, and utilization, angelica stems are typically cut into roughly 4cm sections and blanched in a sugar syrup. Additionally, fresh stems serve as a flavoring agent for liqueurs.

Combatting aphids on angelica flowerheads presents a challenge, with solutions including the introduction of ladybirds or their larvae. Seedlings and young plants, being susceptible to slug and snail predation, warrant protective measures. Furthermore, vigilance against powdery mildew, particularly during dry spells, is essential, necessitating adequate watering to mitigate the risk. In cases of aphid infestation, a forceful hose spray can dislodge the pests, provided beneficial predators are absent.

Angelica encompasses several cultivars, such as Angelica archangelica, Angelica gigas, and Angelica sylvestris. Angelica archangelica, distinguished by its large lime-green flowerheads and pink-flushed stems, stands as the most prevalent variety, revered for its holistic healing properties. Angelica gigas, recognized as Korean angelica, boasts ornamental appeal, featuring smaller, rich purple-hued flower clusters that attract pollinators and serve as exquisite cut flowers. Meanwhile, Angelica sylvestris, though smaller in stature, shares similar attributes albeit with less potent aromatic qualities.

2. Bee Balm, or Bergamot

Bee balm, also referred to as bergamot plant, stands as a perennial herbaceous plant within the mint family, offering ease of cultivation and maintenance. Its vibrant blossoms during summer and medicinal attributes render it invaluable for both human and wildlife use. Originating from North America, bee balm has a historical association with Native American tribes, who utilized it for various medicinal purposes, including treating sore throats, colds, and fever. Presently, bee balm continues to hold significance in herbal medicine, with its leaves serving as a base for teas possessing anti-inflammatory and antiseptic properties.

Cultivating and nurturing bee balm in one's garden proves straightforward, presenting an ideal choice for those seeking to attract wildlife while relishing the beauty of its red, pink, or purple-hued flowers, which serve as a magnet for pollinators. Optimal planting locations include areas with full sun exposure or partial shade, boasting moist yet well-drained soil conditions. During planting, it's advisable to excavate a hole slightly larger than the plant's rootball, gently loosening the roots before insertion. Adequate spacing of approximately 45cm between plants ensures sufficient air circulation. Post-planting, thorough watering is essential to facilitate establishment while maintaining soil moisture.

Maintenance of bee balm remains low-key once established, demanding minimal intervention. Regular watering is advised during dry spells, with mulching around the base aiding moisture retention. Consistent deadheading of flowers promotes prolonged blooming and prevents premature seed production. Optimal positioning entails selecting spots with partial afternoon shade to shield the plant from intense midsummer sunlight.

When grown from seed, bee balm typically reaches its full blooming potential from the second year onward. Pruning is crucial during two primary periods: autumn, upon the demise of top growth, or in late May, with a 'Chelsea Chop' entailing a one-third reduction of the entire plant. Elimination of any dead or diseased foliage serves to curb pest and disease spread.

Although not classified as an invasive species in the UK, periodic monitoring of garden spaces is advised to prevent overgrowth. In instances of excessive spreading, preemptive measures involve plant division and relocation.

Bee balm, characterized by its relatively short lifespan and robust growth, lends itself to propagation through periodic lifting and division of plants. Division in spring entails delicately separating roots into smaller segments. Alternatively, seed germination indoors during midspring, followed by outdoor transplantation post-frost, ensures optimal growth conditions.

Alternatively, spring presents an opportune time for stem cutting, with lower leaf removal and subsequent planting in moist, well-draining compost-filled pots facilitating root establishment. Post-root establishment, transfer the cuttings to larger pots until they attain sufficient size for outdoor planting.

While relatively resilient against pests, bee balm may fall prey to certain insects and diseases. Common pests include aphids and thrips, with natural predators such as birds and wasps serving as effective control agents. In cases of substantial infestation, application of water and dish soap or insecticidal soap sprays proves beneficial, albeit with caution to avoid collateral damage to beneficial predators. Fungal diseases like powdery mildew, prevalent in hot, humid conditions, necessitate preventive measures such as avoiding overhead watering and ensuring adequate air circulation.

When acquiring bee balm, prioritizing reputable suppliers offering healthy, disease-free plants is paramount. Whether purchasing from garden centers or nurseries, a thorough inspection at the point of sale facilitates the selection of robust specimens. Popular varieties include Monarda 'Cambridge Scarlet', Monarda 'Prärienacht', Monarda 'Jacob Cline', Monarda 'Squaw', and Monarda 'Bubblegum Blast'.

3. Echinacea, or Coneflower

Echinacea purpurea, commonly known as purple coneflower, emerges as a resilient perennial plant that has surged in popularity, particularly within prairie-style landscaping trends. Characterized by its charming daisy-like flowers centered around a cone, this herbaceous perennial thrives in most soil types, except overly dry ones. Suited for mass planting within cottage-style or herbaceous borders, or in conjunction with grasses and rudbeckias in prairie-style arrangements, Echinacea purpurea boasts versatility in garden design.

Resilient against inclement weather conditions and free from staking requirements, its enduring flowers, ideal for cutting, attract a myriad of pollinators. A diverse array of cultivars exists, including the shorter 'Magnus', featuring dark pink blossoms, and 'Mistra', sporting shorter, pale pink flowers.

Successful cultivation of Echinacea purpurea entails situating it in well-drained soil with full sun exposure. Deadheading fading flowers promotes continuous blooming, while retention of seedheads in autumn provides nourishment for birds. Spring pruning post-foliage emergence, coupled with autumn mulching using well-rotted manure or compost, ensures robust growth. Congested clumps may be lifted and divided during autumn or spring.

Recognized for its appeal to bees, birds, and other pollinators, Echinacea purpurea poses no reported toxicity risks to animals or humans.

4. Fenugreek

Fenugreek, originating from arid regions surrounding the Mediterranean, holds prominence as a favored culinary ingredient, spice, and medicinal herb. Belonging to the legume family alongside peanuts and beans, it finds widespread usage, particularly in Indian cuisine, where it serves as a staple food component. While not extensively cultivated in U.S. gardens, its flavorful leaves, seeds, and charming flowers warrant broader cultivation.

Thriving in full sun to partial shade and well-draining soil, fenugreek exhibits optimal growth and flowering. Like its leguminous counterparts, it proves advantageous for crop rotation, enhancing soil fertility post-harvest through nutrient-rich decomposition.

For fenugreek cultivation, direct sowing into gardens post-frost risk alleviation in spring, coupled with warm soil conditions, proves ideal. Planting seeds at a depth of approximately 1/4 inch and ensuring adequate watering kickstarts rapid seedling emergence within the initial week.

Key care considerations encompass sun exposure, with provisions for shading in hotter climates, alongside soil drainage and nitrogen availability. While less finicky about soil type compared to non-leguminous varieties, fenugreek contributes to nitrogen fixation. Vigilance against overwatering, which predisposes plants to root rot and subsequent demise, is paramount.

Fenugreek's thriving parameters include warm to hot and arid conditions, necessitating strategic placement, especially in cooler locales, such as against south-facing structures to elevate ambient temperatures. While fertilizer application is optional for moderately depleted soils, enriching the soil with compost or aged manure augments productivity and sets the stage for future plantings.

Pruning, while non-essential, facilitates bushier growth when central growth points are pinched off. Apt deadheading techniques prolong bloom durations.

Pest and disease management entail addressing insect infestations like aphids through organic pesticide application, such as insecticidal soap. Mitigating root rot risks entails soil amendment pre-planting, incorporating sand and compost to bolster drainage.

Fenugreek propagation centers primarily on seeds. Post-drying, seeds are harvested and stored in cool, dark settings until readiness for sowing. Seed pre-treatment involves overnight soaking in water before planting.

While fenugreek poses no toxicity concerns in standard doses, caution is advised for pregnant individuals and those with known peanut allergies.

Optimal leaf utilization precedes flowering to circumvent toughness and diminished palatability.

Given its shallow root system, fenugreek adapts well to pot cultivation and indoor growth, particularly as sprouts and microgreens.

5. Garlic

Cultivating garlic at home proves effortless and space-efficient, demanding minimal effort while yielding satisfying results. Distinguished into softneck and hardneck types, softneck garlic predominates supermarket aisles with its white, papery skin and generous clove count, ideally suited to milder southern UK regions but adaptable with winter safeguards. Conversely, hardneck garlic, denser in texture and bearing fewer cloves, flourishes across the UK, often exhibiting a distinctive 'scape' or flowering stalk that warrants prompt removal to enhance bulb growth. Delaying scape removal may impede bulb development for up to three years.

For those preferring a milder garlic flavor, elephant garlic offers sizable, delicately flavored bulbs. Successful garlic cultivation necessitates a warm, sun-drenched locale with well-draining, moderately moist soil to avoid winter waterlogging. Acquiring bulbs from garden centers or specialized seed suppliers rather than supermarkets ensures optimal planting stock. Planting entails setting large cloves downward with a 2.5cm soil cover over the pointed end. Harvest commences from July onwards, coinciding with the onset of yellowing foliage, followed by sun-drying prior to storage.

While traditionally planted in late autumn or early winter, regions with heavy soil may opt for early spring planting for improved success rates. Planting directly into the ground or initiating growth in small pots accommodates diverse soil conditions, with container cultivation presenting a viable alternative.

Combatting potential challenges, such as bird interference and soil-borne diseases like onion white rot, demands proactive measures like netting or fleece protection post-planting and stringent plant disposal protocols. Minimal care, comprising regular watering until foliage yellows, accompanied by diligent weeding to mitigate competition, suffices for robust garlic growth. Disbudding flowers or scapes prevents diversion of plant energy and is a culinary asset for stir-fry enthusiasts.

Garlic, largely resilient to pests, may occasionally encounter leek rust, necessitating attentive monitoring and early harvesting to avert fungal infestation. Post-harvest, bulbs undergo a brief drying period before storage in cool, dry settings, prioritizing softneck varieties for prolonged preservation.

Harnessing garlic's culinary versatility, preparations range from crushing and slicing to roasting whole cloves, enriching an array of dishes with its pungent aroma. From BBC Good Food's garlic butter recipe to the savory depth of hardneck varieties, garlic offers culinary exploration opportunities aplenty.

Navigating garlic procurement, reputable suppliers like Crocus or Gardeners' World showcase diverse cultivars, from the mild and early maturing Garlic

'Early Purple Wight' to the robust and versatile Garlic 'Christo'. With prudent selection and cultivation practices, home-grown garlic elevates culinary experiences with its distinctive flavor and aromatic charm.

6. Ginger

Ginger, a tropical perennial herb, flourishes in warm climates and can be cultivated as a long-season annual in regions with cooler temperatures. Here are eight essential tips for successfully growing ginger:

1. Understanding Ginger Growth: Ginger originates from rhizomes, which are underground horizontal stems containing multiple buds or growth points. When planted, these rhizomes produce bamboo-like shoots that nourish the developing ginger underground.

2. Purchasing and Preparing Ginger: Obtain ginger from reputable sources such as seed companies or local markets. Cut the rhizomes into 2-3 inch pieces, ensuring each piece has 2 to 3 nodules. Allow the cut ends to dry and form a callus before planting.

3. Allowing Sufficient Growing Time: Ginger requires a prolonged warm growing season of approximately 10 months to thrive. Regions in Zone 8 and above typically offer adequate conditions for outdoor ginger cultivation. Plant rhizomes with the nodules facing upward, burying them 2 inches deep and spacing them 6-8 inches apart. For square foot gardening, allocate 4 ginger rhizomes per square foot.

4. Providing Warmth: Ginger is sensitive to temperatures below 55°F. Choose the warmest available location for planting, considering areas with reflected heat from block walls. Container gardening is advisable in cooler climates, as containers warm up quicker in spring. Indoors, maintain temperatures around 75°F and provide 12-14 hours of supplemental lighting.

5. Offering Shade in Hot Climates: In regions with scorching summers, shield growing ginger from intense sunlight to prevent leaf damage.

Identify naturally shaded areas or create artificial shade to protect the plants.

In essence, ginger is a versatile herb adaptable to diverse climates, thriving in both warm and cool environments. Employing these eight strategies ensures successful ginger cultivation, whether in tropical or temperate regions.

Furthermore, cultivating ginger in containers or herb gardens necessitates nutrient-rich, well-draining soil supplemented with organic matter. Mulching aids in weed suppression and moisture retention, while periodic compost application encourages rhizome growth. For optimal results, consider feeding ginger with organic fertilizers like liquid seaweed or fish emulsion every few weeks.

Correct watering practices are pivotal, particularly during active growth phases, necessitating well-draining soil to prevent waterlogging. Timely harvesting is critical, with colder climates harvesting before frost sets in, while warmer regions wait until foliage yellows and withers before harvesting. In warmer locales, ginger can be grown as a perennial, allowing for year-round harvesting.

Post-harvest, rinse ginger thoroughly, removing shoots and large roots, and utilize the leaves for tea. Store fresh ginger in plastic bags in the refrigerator or freezer, with unpeeled ginger lasting approximately a month in the refrigerator and up to a year in the freezer. Dehydrating ginger involves peeling and slicing before drying at 95°F for 8-12 hours. Store the dehydrated slices in airtight glass jars or process them into powder for extended shelf life.

Finally, processing ginger into powder entails blending young, unpeeled ginger or peeled ginger with water and freezing the mixture in herb or ice cube trays for prolonged storage. By adhering to these guidelines, you can ensure robust ginger growth and a bountiful harvest in your garden.

7. Jasmine

Jasmine, scientifically known as Jasminum spp., is a highly sought-after plant renowned for its captivating fragrance and medicinal properties. While predominantly thriving in tropical to subtropical regions, certain varieties can also flourish in temperate zones, adding a touch of exotic allure to diverse landscapes.

Key to successful jasmine cultivation is safeguarding the plants from cold temperatures. Optimal growth conditions entail selecting a warm, sheltered location with well-draining, moderately fertile soil. Conducting a soil test aids in determining the ideal pH level, while supplementing with high-quality compost facilitates rapid establishment of new plants. Enhancing blooming potential involves applying fertilizer in early spring just before the onset of new growth, with well-balanced granular feeds preferred for their gradual nutrient release over the growing season.

During the peak of summer, jasmine plants necessitate thorough weekly watering, with more frequent watering required for those potted or container-bound. While the plants thrive in consistently moist conditions, vigilance against overwatering is crucial. While most jasmine species thrive in full sun, regions experiencing high heat and humidity may benefit from mid-day shade.

Encouraging robust growth and abundant blooms involves strategic pruning, particularly in the vine's second year, where pinching off stem tips fosters branching and lushness. Deadheading and pruning flowering jasmine immediately after blooming cessation contribute to plant vigor, while indoor jasmine plants slated for overwintering benefit from aggressive pruning.

Propagation offers an avenue for expanding jasmine plantings, with late spring or summer serving as optimal times to commence the process. Stem cuttings from new growth, devoid of excess leaves, can be inserted into trays filled with moist growing medium. While optional, the use of root hormone aids in expedited rooting. Consistent moisture maintenance facilitates rooting, with cuttings typically establishing roots within 4-6 weeks.

While outdoor jasmine plants generally evade pest and disease issues, regular monitoring remains prudent. Indoor overwintered specimens, however, may be susceptible to foliar diseases and pest infestations, necessitating vigilant observation and timely intervention. Horticultural oil or neem oil applications prove effective against pests like spider mites and aphids.

The Jasminum genus encompasses a diverse array of flowering jasmine species, each sharing similarities in appearance and growth requirements. Notable species include Common jasmine (Jasminum officinale), distinguished by its vine morphology and glossy green leaves, Royal jasmine

(Jasminum grandiflorum), and Arabian jasmine (Jasminum sambac), a compact bush adorned with evergreen foliage. Winter jasmine (Jasminum nudiflorum) stands out for its cold-hardiness, although lacking the signature fragrance of other varieties.

In summation, jasmine stands as a versatile and cherished addition to gardens, thriving in various climates with proper care and attention to planting nuances.

8. Lavender

For comprehensive guidance on lavender cultivation, refer to "Growing Lavender for Profit: Make Money from Lavender Business, Uncovering the Benefits, Growing Techniques and Strategies for Massive Profits" by David Werner. This invaluable resource equips lavender enthusiasts with everything necessary for successful lavender cultivation, from growth techniques to harvesting strategies.

9. Lemongrass a fragrant herb with a lemony flavor, originates from tropical climates and is commonly used in Asian cuisine, teas, and various dishes. It adds a refreshing zest to meals and beverages. To cultivate lemongrass, it's vital to protect it from frost. Potted lemongrass plants, known for their tender nature, thrive outdoors during summer but should be moved indoors when winter arrives.

Adequate moisture is crucial for lemongrass, necessitating consistent attention to prevent compost from drying out. While watering should be reduced in winter, the soil should remain slightly moist. Lemongrass can be grown from supermarket stems or seeds, flourishing best in a greenhouse or conservatory with temperatures above 5°C. Alternatively, it can be cultivated outdoors in sunny spots during summer and then transitioned indoors for winter.

Two methods exist for growing lemongrass: from seeds or supermarket-bought stems. Seed cultivation involves sowing thinly on moist compost surfaces without covering them, then maintaining warmth to aid germination. Supermarket stems can also be used by placing them in water until new growth emerges, followed by weekly feeding with liquid fertilizer.

During harvest, stems should be cut just below the base, leaving sufficient foliage for new growth. Preventing lemongrass rust, a result of excessive moisture and humidity, involves regular feeding, pruning of diseased leaves, and avoiding overhead watering. Yellow or brown spots on leaves may indicate the presence of yellow sugarcane aphids, although lemongrass is typically resilient to this pest.

Various lemongrass varieties are available for cultivation from seed, such as Cymbopogon citratus and Cymbopogon flexuosus, obtainable from reputable seed suppliers like Suttons and Mr Fothergills.

10. Red clover (Trifolium pratense), a prevalent true clover species in the UK, offers rapid growth and decent persistence for up to three years. It serves as an excellent soil-improving break crop in arable rotations, boasting a robust tap root that enhances soil structure.

Red clover thrives on most soils, particularly heavier clay soils with a slightly acidic to neutral pH. Optimal sowing times range from April to May in spring and mid-late August in autumn, with the establishment likelihood diminishing if sowing occurs too late into September or too early in spring.

For successful cultivation, red clover seeds should be sown no deeper than 10mm into a newly prepared seedbed. Roll the area well to ensure optimal seed-to-soil contact. As a green manure, red clover can be cut multiple times throughout the season to return green material to the soil.

Grass and clover mixes generally yield more than pure red clover stands, with yields ranging from 6t DM/ha for pure stands to up to 15t DM/ha for grass and clover mixes. However, pure red clover stands are more susceptible to soil-borne diseases like Sclerotinia trifolium and the stem nematode Ditylenchus dipsaci, necessitating a four-year gap between red clover crops to mitigate risks. Other fertility-building crops like white clover can be considered as alternatives.

www.ingramcontent.com/pod-product-compliance
Lightning Source LLC
Chambersburg PA
CBHW070248230526
45470CB00002B/517